THE PROSPERING POWER OF PRAYER

Catherine Ponder

DeVorss Publications
Camarillo, California

The Prospering Power of Prayer
Copyright © 1983 by Catherine Ponder

ISBN13: 978-087516-516-5
Library of Congress Catalog Card Number: 83-70048

DeVorss & Company, Publisher
PO Box 1389
Camarillo CA 93011-1389
www.devorss.com

Other Books by Catherine Ponder

A PROSPERITY LOVE STORY
Memoir

THE DYNAMIC LAWS OF PROSPERITY

THE DYNAMIC LAWS OF HEALING

THE PROSPERITY SECRET OF THE AGES

THE DYNAMIC LAWS OF PRAYER

THE HEALING SECRET OF THE AGES

OPEN YOUR MIND TO PROSPERITY

DARE TO PROSPER

THE SECRET OF UNLIMITED PROSPERITY

OPEN YOUR MIND TO RECEIVE

THE PROSPERING POWER OF PRAYER

The Millionaires of the Bible Series:

THE MILLIONAIRES OF GENESIS

THE MILLIONAIRE MOSES

THE MILLIONAIRE JOSHUA

THE MILLIONAIRE FROM NAZARETH

CONTENTS

Part I: Attitudes of increase. Blessing others brings increase. Bless yourself with the thought of increase. Success in your work. Part II: A deliberate action that leads to increase. How they demonstrated enough to spare and to share. One problem and one solution. The brother who gave. The brother who withheld. The contrast in results. Where you give affects your prosperity.

INTRODUCTION:

LET'S PRAY AND PROSPER

A Message From the Author

A Houston businessman once said to me, "I am successful, yet I have never considered it necessary to pray in order to prosper."

His statement was more one of skepticism than of criticism. Like this man, people are sometimes puzzled at the idea of prospering through prayer. Yet what more logical and normal method is there for succeeding in life? Surely it is easier and more natural to pray and prosper than to fight, scheme, strain and strive to do so. Some authorities claim that what it usually

takes a person six hours to do could easily be ac-
complished in only one hour by a person who
prayed and meditated first.

Perhaps this book is somewhat in answer to
that man's skepticism about the success power
of prayer.

In any event, another businessman recently
wrote from Europe:

> The prospering power of prayer has helped
> me find the courage to start a new business at
> an age when most people are already retired.
> After working twenty years in the executive
> field in Europe, I am now into consulting work.
>
> Today I am sitting in a train returning from
> Lugano, in the Italian-speaking part of Switz-
> erland, where I have just found the answer to
> one of my prayers: An apartment as a first step
> to moving my home and business headquarters
> into southern Switzerland.
>
> Another prayer was answered yesterday: Fly-
> ing from Amsterdam to Zurich, I found myself
> sitting next to a senior banker who is on the
> board of a firm to which I had been seeking an
> introduction for months! I am convinced that
> the poet was right: "More things are wrought
> by prayer than this world dreams of."

A businesswoman in Indiana recently reported, "I met my husband six months ago. He

is exactly what I had pictured in prayer for several years. We are very happy—a match made in heaven."

Still another lady wrote from Arizona:

> So many changes have happened in my life since I began using affirmative prayer, and prayer through pictures. I feel a much deeper sense of peace in my soul. I look forward to my morning meditations and daily periods of inspirational study. Both inner and outer changes are taking place.
>
> I spent so long trying to run my life by myself, and feeling frustrated over things that seemed beyond my control. Now I've put my life in God's hands and I am receiving more riches than I had previously imagined possible —emotionally, financially and physically.

Perhaps a fifteen-year-old said it best: "The belief that one can pray and prosper makes life what it should be: exciting and full of enjoyment. God didn't put us here to be poor and stay on the ground. He wants us to reach for the stars and be prosperous."

Amen!

I invite you to join me and countless people on a worldwide basis who are practicing the prospering power of prayer. As more and more people take up this soul-satisfying method for meeting life victoriously, it can become the answer to mankind's needs on every level of life.

So together let us dare to pray and prosper.

Catherine Ponder

P.O. Drawer 1278
Palm Desert, California, 92261
U.S.A.

THE SIMPLE FORMS OF PRAYER THAT CAN PROSPER YOU

You are prosperous to the degree that you are experiencing peace, health, and plenty in your world. *Prayer can help you experience peace, health, and plenty, because prayer is man's steady effort to know God, and God is the source of all man's good. Thus, in prayer man makes common union with God and His infinite goodness.*

It is wonderful, too, to realize that prayer is natural to man, and not a strange, mysterious practice. *Man has always prayed and always will.* In his primitive understanding, man prayed to the sun and stars, to fire and water, to animals and plants, to images and myths. Later, as the intellect of man evolved, his ideas changed and he envisioned God as a personal deity with sentiments and emotions—a God with human traits, a God man felt had to be appeased by sacrificial offerings and assailed with pleas for favor. Many of the writers of the Old Testament had this concept of God. Still later, mankind began to come out of a primitive and intellectual understanding of God into a spiritual awareness that God is not a hostile being with a split personality of good and evil, but a God of love, the unchanging Principle of supreme good, both within and around mankind. *Methods of prayer that have evolved, expanded, and improved now make it easy to pray to and commune with God.*

Brother Lawrence, sixteenth-century French lay brother, who believed greatly in the power of prayer, described his method of prayer as "practicing the presence of God." One biographer has written that Brother Lawrence's one single aim was to bring about a conscious personal union between himself and God and that he took the "shortest cut he could find to accomplish it." And what was his short cut to God? Brother Lawrence described it thus: "The time of business does not with me differ from the time of prayer; and in the noise and clutter of my kitchen, while several persons are at the same time calling for different things, I possess God in as great tranquility as if I were upon my knees at the blessed sacrament." At any moment, in the midst of any occupation, under any circumstances, the soul that wants to know God can "practice the presence."

THE POWER OF PRAYER TO PROSPER

The one who understands the true nature of God as a rich, loving Father soon realizes that *the person who truly prays is bound to succeed, because he attunes himself to the richest, most powerful, most successful force in the universe.* Jesus knew this when He promised, "All things whatsoever ye shall ask in prayer, believing, ye shall receive." (Matthew 21:22) Tennyson knew it when he wrote,

"More things are wrought by prayer
Than this world dreams of!"

Many people have not employed the power of prayer for prosperity and success because they have gotten the erroneous idea that it is wrong to pray for material things. However, as many of the Biblical promises indicate, it is right and proper that we should pray for the things we need. We live in a rich, friendly universe that desires to fulfill our needs; and prayer is but an act of faith that helps open channels for the fulfillment of our needs.

The Bible is filled with examples of prayers and requests for needful things. Abraham prayed for a son; David prayed for his household; Elijah prayed for rain; Ezekiel prayed for the people; Hannah prayed for a son; Jehoshaphat prayed for deliverance; Jeremiah prayed for freedom from a famine; Nehemiah prayed for protection; Solomon prayed for wisdom. On a number of occasions, Jesus prayed definitely for specific things.

Praying for things is not the only form of prayer, but if we first begin to pray by praying for things (as most of us do), we will learn the power of prayer; and we will then doubtless develop our prayer power further.

THE FIRST TYPE OF PRAYER: GENERAL PRAYER

Basically, there are four types of prayer: general prayer, the prayer of denial, the prayer of affirmation, and the prayer of meditation and silence. At various times it is good to know and use these four types of prayer to meet life's various needs. The first three are simple methods that can prosper you. The fourth type of prayer, described in the next chapter, is considered by some to be a more advanced method of prayer.

General prayer is the act of praying to God as a loving, understanding Father, in your own way. It can be done on your knees, or more comfortably. It can be expressed through words, or silently. You can have a prayer book before you, or you can browse through your Bible, dwell upon favorite passages and promises.

THE LORD'S PRAYER

A simple, effective way to begin a general prayer is to take the Lord's Prayer and ponder each line of it silently or aloud. The ancients believed that the Lord's Prayer was all powerful, and they often declared it over and over, from twelve to fifteen times, without stopping. At various times in the past, at the shrine of Lourdes, some of those seeking healing were taught to pray the Lord's Prayer fifteen times, while they entered the waters. From my own experiences, I know that deep spiritual power is contacted, brought alive, and released when one prays the Lord's Prayer over and over, either silently or verbally. I have known a number of instances where "hard conditions" in business affairs, human relations problems, and health conditions were adjusted when one or more persons prayed the Lord's Prayer from twelve to fifteen times daily.

CALL UPON THE NAMES JESUS CHRIST, JEHOVAH, AND JEHOVAH-JIREH

Another powerful way to make contact with spiritual power in general prayer is to take the name *Jehovah* from the Old Testament or the name *Jesus Christ* from the New Testament, and verbally or silently declare the name over and over. A housewife told me that her husband became very successful in business (after a number of previous failures) when she began daily to call upon and dwell upon the name *Jehovah* in her prayer times.

A reader in Texas wrote:

A friend of mine was having financial problems. I suggested she begin declaring daily the old Hebrew prayer for prosperity, "JEHOVAH-JIREH, THE LORD RICHLY PROVIDES FOR ME NOW." She soon demonstrated $1,200! It came from a channel through which she had expected to receive only $300 at most.

As for the power of calling on the name *Jesus Christ*, Charles Fillmore has written: "The mightiest vibration is set up by speaking of the name *Jesus Christ*. This is the name that is named 'far above all rule, and authority,' the name above all names, holding in itself all power in heaven and in earth. It is the name that has power to mold the universal substance . . . and when spoken it sets forces into activity that bring results. 'Whatsoever ye shall ask of the Father in my name, he may give it to you.' 'If ye shall ask anything in my name, that will I do.' "[1]

An immigrant once related to me how he was released from a concentration camp, where he had been badly treated, after he began daily calling upon the name *Jesus Christ*. A Christian missionary he met in prison suggested that he pray in this way. At the time, he was supposed to be near death from the many beatings he had received, but instead he began to recover. As he continued dwelling upon this name in his prayers, it was as though a mighty power went to work for him. In a short time, he was released, without explanation, from the concentration

1. Charles Fillmore, *Prosperity* (Unity Village, Mo.: Unity Books, 1936).

camp, even though many of his fellow prisoners were still held and mistreated. As he continued dwelling upon the name of Jesus Christ, further events occurred so that he was able to come to America, where he has lived for a number of happy, grateful years.

"THY WILL BE DONE"

Another powerful way to pray is simply to declare, as in the Lord's Prayer, "Thy will be done," since God's will for us is always un-limited good. A musician was out of work. The band with which he worked had been asked to go to Florida. Upon arrival, the promised job did not materialize, and all the members of the band were stranded. This man prayed, "Father, let Thy supreme good will be done in this mat-ter." One day he and the other members of the band were at union headquarters, hoping that something would turn up, when their agent tele-phoned from New York to say he had located a job for them in Texas.

LET GO AND LET GOD

Another form of general prayer is the prayer of release, of letting go and letting God. When one has "done all," it is good to stand in faith through the prayer of release. A woman was in her farm home in a dense forest area, her husband away on a business trip, when a forest fire broke out. The fire raged all around her property; being surrounded, she could not leave. She prayed, "Father, it's up to You to save me, our house and property. There's nothing more I can do." She then affirmed, "I LET GO AND LET GOD HAVE HIS PERFECT WAY." With a feeling of peace, she released the matter and retired for the night. The next morning she awoke early, to find only a few stumps still burning. The fire had burned right up to her property lines, and stopped. It seemed a miracle. Later in the day when the forest ranger arrived, he said: "There is only one explanation for this. You must have been praying."

You may feel that your prayer experiences have not been particularly satisfying or powerful, or that nothing much has ever happened as a result of your prayers. If so, perhaps it is because you need to develop the other three types of prayer, along with general prayer.

THE SECOND TYPE OF PRAYER: PRAYER OF DENIAL

The second type is one that all business people should know about, because they can use it so helpfully as they go about their business. It is the prayer of denial. Many people cringe at the word *denial*, thinking that its only meaning is restriction or limitation. But the word *deny* also means "to reject as a false conception." And prayers of denial are for that purpose: to reject as a false conception that which is not satisfying or good in one's life experiences. Many hundreds of years before the time of Jesus, the Egyptians used the power of denial through the sign of the cross, indicating a crossing out or blotting out of apparent evil.

Prayers of denial are your "no" prayers. They help you to refuse to accept things as they are, to dissolve your negative thoughts about them and thus make way for something better. Prayers of denial are expressed in those attitudes of mind that say: "I will not put up with or tolerate this experience as necessary, lasting, or right. I refuse to accept things as they are; I mentally claim my whole good, knowing that even now it is manifesting." How much mankind needs to use prayers of denial! So many people lead a pygmy existence of fear, compromise, and dissatisfaction when they might be living lives of gigantic good, if they only knew how to say no to less than the best.

THE THIRD TYPE OF PRAYER: "YES" PRAYERS

Usually, prayers of denial should be followed up by prayers of the third type: prayers of affirmation or "yes" attitudes. It is good to follow up thoughts of what you do not want with thoughts of what you *do* want; to follow up, "No, I will not accept this" with, "Yes, I will accept this or something better."

Jesus said, "Let your speech be, Yea, yea; Nay, nay." (Matthew 5:37) Prayers of denial and affirmation are as much attitudes of mind as they are formal methods of prayer. We can express them silently or verbally wherever we are, either as formal prayers or informally, as attitudes of mind. Charles Fillmore has written that "concentrated attention of the mind on an idea of any kind is equal to prayer, and will make available the spiritual principle that is its source in proportion to the intensity and continuity of the mental effort."[2] In other words, our attitudes are forms of prayer.

2. Fillmore, *Prosperity*.

HOW TO USE "YES" AND "NO" PRAYERS

The prophet Hosea went into more detail to show how to use denial and affirmative prayer power. He advised, "Take with you words, and return unto Jehovah: say unto him, Take away all iniquity, and accept that which is good." (Hosea 14:2) In any situation that is dissatisfying we can deny its power by declaring to a loving Father, "Take away all iniquity." We should then follow up with the affirmation, "I WILL ACCEPT ONLY THAT WHICH IS GOOD."

To dissolve especially troublesome problems or hard conditions, it is necessary to concentrate fully upon prayers of denial before giving much attention to affirmative prayers. I once knew a very negative, disagreeable, complaining person with whom I had to work. As far as she was concerned, nothing was right in her world or in the world generally. She was in ill health; she was always battling out things with her family; she was not properly appreciated or compensated on her job; life was "a mess." I offered her some literature on successful living. She liked it, she said. Sometime when she felt better, got through fighting with her family, had schemed properly to get a raise, she planned to read it. In the meantime, she did not care to be distracted from her practice of negative thinking.

The prayer of denial I used was: "THERE IS
NOTHING BUT GOD'S LOVE AND HARMONY AT WORK
HERE." I hoped that she would subconsciously
attune herself to these ideas of love and harmony and let them work for her. In a short time
she decided to take another job, and left. The
secretary who replaced her was one of the most
joyous, harmonious people I have ever met, and
delightful to work with. Thus, love and harmony appeared when all else was denied.

PRAYERS OF DENIAL WORK FOR YOUR GOOD

So many persons get the erroneous idea that
somebody else can keep their good from them;
they go through life thinking this. Prayers of
denial can dissolve this false belief and the lack
that it causes. Declare: "I DISSOLVE IN MY OWN
MIND, AND IN THE MINDS OF ALL OTHERS, ANY
IDEA THAT MY OWN GOOD CAN BE WITHHELD FROM
ME. THAT WHICH IS FOR MY HIGHEST GOOD NOW
COMES TO ME THROUGH GOD'S GRACE, AND I WEL-
COME IT." This prayer of denial can also clear
up old conditions of the past, where one's good
seemed to have been taken away or withheld.

Another prayer of denial that is helpful when
there seem to be barriers or obstacles on your
pathway is: "ALL BARRIERS AND OBSTACLES TO MY

DIVINELY GIVEN GOOD ARE NOW DISSOLVED, WITH GOD'S HELP." After using this statement for a time, you will find that whereas before, people, situations, and conditions seemed to work against you, everything will shift; everything will begin working *for* you. Still another powerful prayer of denial for clearing away negation is: "THE POWER OF GOD IS WORKING THROUGH ME TO FREE ME FROM EVERY NEGATIVE INFLUENCE. NOTHING CAN HOLD ME IN BONDAGE. ALL POWER IS GIVEN UNTO ME FOR GOOD IN MIND, BODY, AND AFFAIRS, AND I RIGHTLY USE IT HERE AND NOW."

If people only knew to say no to unhappy experiences, rather than to bow down to them! The Hebrews were warned not to bow down to or worship false idols or gods. The gods of unhappiness, dissatisfaction and limitation are among the major heathen gods of today. To dissolve their appearance in your life, declare often: "THERE IS NOTHING FOR ME TO FEAR. GOD'S SPIRIT OF GOOD IS AT WORK AND DIVINE RESULTS ARE NOW COMING FORTH."

AFFIRM NEW GOOD

When you use denials you erase, dissolve, undo. You should then make firm new good, through affirmative prayer. A traveling salesman who was heavily in debt attempted to get a loan from a bank to pay off his debts. Because he lacked adequate collateral, he was not able to get the loan. He began to affirm: "GOD PROSPERS ME NOW." Within a few days he made a large sale and was able to pay off all his debts, with ample money left over. A businesswoman who was greatly depressed went to a mental hospital for treatment. While doctors were still taking tests to determine the proper treatment, a relative began to affirm daily: "PERFECT LOVE CASTS OUT FEAR AND DEPRESSION." Within a short time, this woman's depression had dissolved, and she was released and went back to work.

Several years ago a retired sea captain told me that he was healed of alcoholism after he began using the power of affirmation. He affirmed daily: "I AM BEING HEALED, WITH GOD'S HELP." After a time, he began affirming, "PRAISE GOD, I AM HEALED."

AN ADVANCED FORM OF PRAYER THAT CAN PROSPER YOU

— Chapter 2 —

A friend commented, "It takes self-discipline to succeed." How true. Then she added, " And I am getting better at it." What some consider an advanced form of prayer, the practice of meditation and silence, is a form of self-discipline that can help you to succeed in every phase of your life.

A businessman said, "Getting in tune with God, through the daily practice of meditation and silence, is a lot more fun than I expected."

Another friend reported:

This is my seventieth birthday and the best one yet—such a contrast to my life only a few

16

years ago. After being deserted by my former husband, I was financially destitute and very hurt. Through my practice of daily prayer, meditation, and inspirational study, I happily remarried within a year.

My husband has provided me with a beautiful home and both financial and emotional security. What a change from those years that were filled with so much unhappiness and uncertainty. It is true that "the longer your good is in coming, the greater it will be when it comes," so persevere in your practice of prayer, meditation and inspirational study.

THE FOURTH TYPE OF PRAYER: MEDITATION AND SILENCE

The fourth type of prayer is that of meditation and silence. It is often in silent, contemplative prayer that we feel the presence of God's goodness most strongly. In this form of prayer, we take a few prayerful words and think about them, silently. As we think about them, they grow in our minds as expanded ideas, moving us to a feeling of peaceful assurance and right ideas (and perhaps later, to right action). If nothing seems to happen in meditation, we have nevertheless made our minds receptive to God's good, which may manifest later.

The Psalmist knew the power of the prayer of meditation and silence when he declared, " Be still and know that I am God." (Psalms 46:10) A businessman recently stated that a restless, sleepless night turned into restful sleep after he began meditating upon the Psalmist's words. Dr. Alexis Carrel has described the power of meditation: "When our activity is set toward a precise end, our mental and organic functions become completely harmonized. The unification of the desires, the application of the mind to a single purpose, produce a sort of inner peace. Man integrates himself by meditation, just as by action."[1]

Jesus was constantly going "up into the mountain to pray." After much activity, He often retreated for a time of silent prayer and meditation, to reintegrate Himself. The prophet Haggai pointed out the power of prayer and meditation to the Hebrews after their return from Babylonian exile. They found the Holy City in ruins, poverty-stricken, and surrounded by hostile tribes. *Haggai pointed out the futility of trying to produce outer results without first making inner contact with God*: "Consider your ways. Ye have sown much, and bring in little; ye

---

1. Carrel, *Man the Unknown* (New York: Harper & Brothers, 1935) p. 146.

eat, but ye have not enough; ye drink, but ye
are not filled with drink; ye clothe you, but
there is none warm; and he that earneth wages
earneth wages to put it into a bag with holes."
Then Jehovah told them: "Consider your ways.
Go up to the mountain, and bring wood, and
build the house; and I will take pleasure in it."
(Haggai 1:5-8)

In metaphysical language, the word *mountain* means a high place in thought, feeling, and
prayer. When one gets back to that high place
of peace and power in silent prayer and meditation, one accumulates "wood" — the substance
of new thought, new energy, new power, new
ideas — and is then able to "build the house," or
produce the outer, visible results of good.

Moses, Elijah, and Jesus, among others, proved
the practical, result-getting power of silent
meditation. It was at the conclusion of Moses'
forty-day period of prayer in the wilderness that
he went forth and supervised the construction of
the tabernacle, the Hebrews' first building of
formal worship. Moses even received specific instructions about the rich, beautiful furnishings
for this tabernacle from Jehovah, during his
forty-day meditation period. At the conclusion
of Elijah's forty days of prayer, he knew that
Elisha was to become the next prophet of Israel;
he also anointed a new king over Syria and one

over Israel, to clear up the political confusion of that era. And it was after Jesus had prayed silently and meditated for forty days that he began to preach, heal, and teach.

HOW TO MEDITATE

In her book, *Lessons in Truth,*[2] H. Emilie Cady has described the power of meditation: "Every man must take time daily for quiet meditation. In daily meditation lies the secret of power. . . . You may be so busy with the doing, the outgoing of love to help others (which is unselfish and godlike as far as it goes), that you find no time to go apart. But the command. or rather the invitation, is 'Come ye yourselves apart . . . and rest a while.' (Mark 6:31) And it is the only way in which you will ever gain definite knowledge, true wisdom, newness of experience, steadiness of purpose, or power to meet the unknown, which must come in all daily life."

She also tells how to meditate: "When you withdraw from the world for meditation, let it not be to think of yourself or your failures, but invariably to get all your thoughts centered on

2. Published 1894, revised 1953, by Unity School of Christianity, Unity Village, Missouri, 64065.

God and on your relation to the Creator and
Upholder of the universe. Let all the little an-
noying cares and anxieties go for a while, and
by effort, if need be, turn your thoughts away
from them to some of the simple words of the
Nazarene, or of the Psalmist. Think of some
Truth statement, be it ever so simple. No person, unless he has practiced it, can know how it
quiets all physical nervousness, all fear, all over-
sensitiveness, all the little raspings of everyday
life — just this hour of calm, quiet waiting alone
with God. Never let it be an hour of bondage,
but always one of restfulness."

The Psalmist described meditation and silence as the "secret place of the Most High."
(Psalms 91:1) Jesus spoke of it as going into the
closet and shutting the door (Matt. 6:6). Carlyle
wrote: "Consider the significance of silence; it is
boundless, never by meditating to be ex-
hausted, unspeakably profitable to thee! Cease
that chaotic hubbub, wherein thy soul runs to
waste, to confused suicidal dislocation and stu-
por; *out of silence comes thy strength.*"

HOW MEDITATION RELATES
TO YOUR PROBLEMS

After meditating upon God's goodness and
being renewed, uplifted, and inspired with new

ideas, there is an effective way to utilize meditation and silence in relation to your problems: Take any problem or question and meditate on this thought: "THERE IS A DIVINE SOLUTION TO THIS SITUATION. I ACCEPT AND CLAIM THE DIVINE SOLUTION IN THIS SITUATION NOW." The mental energy spent in worry and battling with the problem will then be used constructively to give you the right ideas and right solution. When you have a problem, if you will go into silent meditation and contemplate its solution from a divine standpoint, you will be shown what to do.

EXECUTIVE SOLVES PROBLEMS THROUGH MEDITATION

An engineering executive has told me of his use of meditation as a problem-solver. When his employees run into difficulty on an engineering project, he goes into his office, silently meditates on the problem from a divine standpoint, and inevitably gets the right ideas for its solution. One of his junior executives once asked him how he managed always to have the right answer just when it was needed most. When he explained his simple method, the junior executive skeptically asked, "You mean you just meditate on the solution, rather than fight the problem?" The engineering executive believes that the world is full of harried, tense people who have become that way through trying to solve problems in outer ways.

LET PRAYER SOLVE YOUR PROBLEMS

Let the practice of prayer, in one of the four forms described in these two chapters, help you solve life's problems in inner, true ways.

Let communion with God and His goodness open the way for greater peace, health and plenty in you and in your world. The writer of the Third Epistle of John might have been describing the prospering power of all of these forms of prayer when he declared, "Beloved, I pray that in all things thou mayest prosper and be in health, even as thy soul prospereth." (3 John 2)

MAKING THE RIGHT CONTACT FOR PROSPERITY

In this era when success is sometimes considered to be the result of knowing the "right people" or having the "right contacts," it is refreshing to read these words of Charles Fillmore: "What we need to realize above all else is that God has provided for the most minute needs of our daily life and that if we lack anything it is because we have not used our mind in making the right contact with the supermind. . . . The spiritual substance from which comes all visible wealth is never depleted.

It is right with you all the time and responds to your faith in it and your demands upon it."[1]

True prosperity, then, is the result of making contact with the spiritual substance within the God-mind of man. Furthermore, that substance will respond to our faith in it and our demands upon it.

Perhaps the most powerful method of making this contact, and yet one of the simpliest, is through affirmative prayer — one of the methods mentioned in Chapter 1. I am devoting an entire chapter to affirmative prayer because it is one of the easiest forms of prayer for many people to use, and it is a favorite form of prayer that has worked miracles in my own life over the years.

HOW TO HAVE ANY GOOD THING

We can have any good thing for which we are willing to pay the price of daily, consistent affirmation. But knowing "about" the power of affirmative prayer isn't enough; we have to *pray* affirmatively, personally and constantly. Our

---

1. Fillmore, *Prosperity.*

words are loaded with power, and every word we speak goes out and returns as a multiplied result. Knowing this, I like to affirm often, "MY WORDS ARE CHARGED WITH PROSPERING POWER."

PRAYING AFFIRMATIVELY BY BLESSING

There are various types of affirmative prayers that we may speak in making the right contact with the God-mind within us. To affirm is simply "to make firm," and affirmative prayers do just that — they make firm our good and help us experience it. One type of affirmative prayer is that of blessing. By blessing the substance at hand, we increase its flow and its immediate multiplying power. If a purse seems empty, we should take it in our hands and bless it by affirming, "I BLESS YOU AND BLESS YOU FOR THE RICHES OF GOD THAT ARE NOW BEING DEMONSTRATED IN AND THROUGH YOU." As we eat our meals, it is good to bless our food. When we dress, we should bless our clothes.

AFFIRMATIONS OF THANKS
PROVE POWERFUL

Here are some of the affirmative prayers that I have used daily — for perfect clothes: "I GIVE

THANKS THAT I AM APPROPRIATELY AND DIVINELY CLOTHED WITH THE RICH SUBSTANCE OF GOD"; for a perfect home: "I GIVE THANKS THAT I AM APPROPRIATELY AND DIVINELY HOUSED WITH THE RICH SUBSTANCE OF GOD"; for perfect transportation: "I GIVE THANKS THAT I AM APPROPRIATELY AND DIVINELY TRANSPORTED, WHEREVER I WISH TO GO, WITH THE RICH SUBSTANCE OF GOD."

Many businesswomen particularly like this affirmation: "I GIVE THANKS FOR EVER-INCREASING HEALTH, YOUTH, AND BEAUTY, IN THE NAME OF JESUS CHRIST." Other affirmations of thanks that have proved powerful for many people are these—for increased income: "I GIVE THANKS THAT MY FINANCIAL INCOME INCREASES MIGHTILY NOW, THROUGH THE DIRECT ACTION OF GOD"; for payment of indebtedness and financial obligations: "I GIVE THANKS FOR THE IMMEDIATE, COMPLETE PAYMENT OF ALL FINANCIAL OBLIGATIONS, IN THE NAME OF JESUS CHRIST"; for increased success along all lines: "I GIVE THANKS THAT EVERY DAY IN EVERY WAY I AM GROWING RICHER AND RICHER."

HARMONY AND PROSPERITY IN
HOME AND BUSINESS

Recently a group of Truth students were asked to affirm the following prayer for har-

mony in their homes and businesses: "LET
THERE BE PEACE WITHIN MY WALLS AND PROSPER-
ITY WITHIN MY PALACES." They reported happy,
peaceful results.

This same group was asked to affirm for new
business and new customers: "I LOVE THE HIGH-
EST AND BEST IN ALL PEOPLE AND I NOW DRAW THE
HIGHEST AND BEST PEOPLE [CUSTOMERS, CLIENTS]
TO ME." This prayer seemed to "click" with the
entire group and produced exciting experiences. A salesman discovered that by speaking
this prayer, he attracted into his department
only people who really intended to buy and who
did buy. Consistent use of this prayer also
helped him to make a number of sales that he
previously thought he had lost.

Another member of this group, a saleswoman
who is employed in a store with more than a
hundred employees, prayed this prayer with
such great success that she led the entire store in
sales. She was honored by her employers for
having sold $44,000 worth of merchandise with-
in a given period. Only three other salespeople
in that store (all men) sold more than $30,000
worth of merchandise during the same period.
This woman's department was one of the lower-
priced merchandise areas, which necessitated
her making more individual sales.

AFFIRMATIVE PRAYERS BRING ABUNDANCE

Another affirmative prayer that this group found helpful was: "EVERYTHING AND EVERYBODY PROSPERS ME NOW." A government employee who spoke this prayer daily was soon informed of an inheritance that had been available but unclaimed for a number of years. Another Unity student who was praying this prayer was one of eleven heirs who inherited a gravel pit in another state. Because of the number of heirs, the amount of money she received from this inheritance had been small. After faithfully affirming, "EVERYTHING AND EVERYBODY PROSPERS ME NOW," her income checks from the gravel business began arriving monthly in larger and larger amounts. During the winter months, when this business was supposed to "slump," she received the largest income of all. She now has an increasing monthly income from her inheritance.

The owner of a modeling school formed a chain of charm and modeling schools as a result of her successful use of affirmative prayer. She discovered after using this same prayer that she felt led to teach fewer classes than in the past. However, class attendance was larger and her classes were comprised of prosperous-minded students who paid for their courses on time or even ahead of time. Consequently her income steadily increased.

One housewife had long hoped to make a trip to Hawaii, to visit relatives stationed there with the armed forces. After affirming, "EVERYTHING AND EVERYBODY PROSPERS ME NOW," not only did the way open for her to make the trip but her husband, a businessman, was also able to arrange a month away from his job. Together they flew to Hawaii and had a glorious month with their family.

After using this same affirmative prayer, a secretary felt led to sell and reinvest some securities she had inherited several years previously but which had not brought adequate compensation. After reinvesting them, she received immediate financial return on her securities.

PRAISE AS PRAYER

Still another form of affirmative prayer is sincere praise. We should praise what we have, and in our thoughts and words we should insist that it is constantly expanding into greater good. We should also praise God for His goodness that is always at work in our lives. George Muller, who has been described as "the man of faith to whom God gave millions," once said: "Expect great things of God and great things you will have. There is no limit to what He is able to do. Praise Him for everything. I have praised Him many times when He sent me ten cents and I have praised Him when He has sent me sixty thousand dollars. I have trusted Him for one dollar and I have trusted Him for thousands, and never in vain."

A wonderful way to express praise is to begin the day by affirming prosperity and success, instead of facing it with dread, fear, or tense anxiety. Praise has a happy, relaxing effect upon us and our world. In the early morning hours, send praise ahead of you into the day and insure its success by affirming: "WITH PRAISE AND THANKSGIVING, I SET THE RICHES OF GOD BEFORE ME THIS DAY TO GUIDE, GOVERN, PROTECT, AND PROSPER ME. ALL THINGS NEEDFUL ARE NOW PROVIDED. MY RICH GOOD BECOMES VISIBLE THIS DAY!"

THE PROSPERING POWER OF CONFIDENCE

A stockbroker recently brought to my attention another type of affirmative prayer that helps him make the right contact for prosperity: affirmations of confidence. He stated that he has studied the prosperity law from every angle, observed the many prosperous-minded people who buy and sell stock, and read many biographies of the lives of prosperous-minded people. He has come to the conclusion that if prosperity could be described in one word, that word would be *self-confidence;* that is, confidence in one's abilities and talents, and in God's help in developing them.

Affirmative prayers that express confidence help us release our prosperity powers. Psychologists tell us that there is tremendous power in having self-confidence. They say that *confidence doubles our powers and multiplies our abilities.* We may more fully develop the prosperity power of confidence by affirming often, "I AM CONFIDENT THAT GOD IS MY INSTANT, CONSTANT, ABUNDANT SUPPLY OF HEALTH, WEALTH AND HAPPINESS," or, "I AM THE RICHLY ILLUMINED CHILD OF GOD, FILLED WITH DIVINE LOVE AND WISDOM, BY WHICH I AM GUIDED IN ALL MY WAYS AND NOW LED INTO THAT WHICH IS FOR MY HIGHEST GOOD."

A SUCCESSFUL REPAIR PLAN

A railroad employee was asked to repair a locomotive that no one else had been able to adjust. When he heard of the various mechanics who had attempted to repair this engine without success, he was almost overwhelmed. But then he remembered the power of affirmative prayer. Before beginning work, he went aside to a quiet place and from his wallet he took this affirmation and spoke it silently: "I AM A CHILD OF THE LIVING GOD. I AM ONE WITH HIS WISDOM; THAT WISDOM NOW LEADS ME IN PATHS OF RIGHTEOUSNESS, PEACE, AND TRUE SUCCESS." As he was thinking of these words and letting them fill him with confidence, another employee passed through the shop and asked what he was doing, to which he replied that he was "going over a plan" that he intended to use in repairing the locomotive. Shortly thereafter, he returned to his work and quickly repaired the troublesome engine. Later the other employee asked him for a copy of the "plan" he had used with such quick success.

BUSINESSMAN AFFIRMS "NONRETIREMENT"

A certain executive was within a year of retirement, yet he did not feel that he was ready for a rocking chair. So he began praying that other divinely satisfying work would open to him. Since he did not know just what outer contacts to make to help bring forth such a result, he made none. Instead, he made the inner contact by spending a lot of time quietly affirming this prayer of confidence: "THE SPIRIT OF THE LORD GOES BEFORE ME, MAKING EASY AND SUCCESSFUL MY WAY."

One day he received a telephone call from someone he had never met, offering him work in Florida, of the same type he had been handling. Within a week, he received a similar offer by mail. *Prayers of confidence multiply not only our powers and our abilities, but also our opportunities.* Within a short time, this man resigned his job, sold his home, and made the change into a new position that holds a limitless future for him — because he dared to affirm confidently, "THE SPIRIT OF THE LORD GOES BEFORE ME, MAKING EASY AND SUCCESSFUL MY WAY."

THE RIGHT CONTACT FOR PROSPERITY

If you have a prosperity need, be assured that you can make the "right contact" for prosperity. God has provided for the most minute needs of your daily life. If you lack anything, use your mind to make the right contact with the supermind of God within you. A postal employee who had to take an efficiency test affirmed, "DIVINE

MIND KNOWS AND DIVINE MIND SHOWS." His test proved him most efficient.

Affirmative prayers that express praise, thanks, blessing, confidence, and rich ideas of good are powerful yet simple channels for making the right contact with the supermind of God within you for prosperity.

THE POTENT PRAYERS OF PRAISE AND THANKSGIVING

— Chapter 4 —

Most of us have not realized the potent power that lies in prayers of praise and thanksgiving. They are miracle workers.

The secret of harvesting our good is to begin to praise God and to give thanks *before* our joy and other forms of good actually appear. *If we wait for things to happen before we praise and give thanks, we may wait indefinitely.*

As spiritual beings, we should gain control of circumstances, events, and our own reactions to personalities. As spiritual beings we have the power to create our own circumstances, events, and environment. The secret is to sing, to rejoice, to praise, and to give thanks even *before* there seems to be anything for which to give thanks.

A housewife, who had been a chronic grumbler, said that she stumbled on the potent power of the prayer of praise through the trial-and-error method. Her use of praise not only healed her body of pain, it healed her mind. She said:

> I have proved to my satisfaction that praise will work along all lines. I have known praise to change even the face of nature, and to work what the ignorant call a miracle.

Most of us have seen the effect that praise has on animal and plant life. My mother talked to and praised potted plants that were everywhere in her house. I always considered this one of mother's little habits, but now I know that her use of the spiritual principle of praise and blessing was her secret with her flowers. This secret caused her neighbors to often say that she had a green thumb.

THE HEALING POWER OF PRAISE

We can harvest our good through prayers of praise, because *words that express praise, thanks, and gratitude release energies within our minds and bodies.* When we release energy through praise, we can be strong in body instead of weak. We can have peace and trust instead of fear, and we can have poise and power instead of shattered nerves. Myrtle Fillmore, wife, mother and former school-teacher, who became the co-founder of the Unity movement, talked to, blessed and praised her body temple constantly for two years. She finally brought forth health where there had been diagnosis of an incurable disease.

From South Carolina a reader has reported:

> I had had back trouble for twenty years. Then I learned of the miraculous power of praise. I began to declare, I PRAISE GOD I AM HEALED NOW. After five days of affirming these words, the soreness and pain left my back. I am ashamed to admit I was surprised.
>
> In addition to the freedom from pain, I also still have the $60 to $70 that it would have cost me for doctor's bills. What blessings praise hath wrought!

Our thoughts and words of praise can also do much to help others.

A housewife from Illinois wrote:

I stayed last night with a friend whose husband had been taken by ambulance to the hospital a few days ago in a comatose state. Three physicians stated his symptoms indicated a brain tumor of a malignant nature. All three doctors predicted he would not live long enough for tests to be made.

Before going to bed around midnight last night, his wife and I studied an inspirational pamphlet which described the miraculous power of praise and thanksgiving. Together we spoke words of praise and thanksgiving for her husband's immediate healing.

At 3:30 A.M. she telephoned the intensive care unit at the hospital to inquire about her husband. The nurse reported he had opened his eyes, that he had answered her questions, and that he had moved his arms and legs upon request.

This morning the nurses reported that oxygen was no longer needed. The patient was breathing naturally and was to be moved out of intensive care this afternoon. Meanwhile, their son—who believed the three doctors' previous diagnosis—had completed the funeral arrangements! All of us are now giving thanks for the miraculous healing power that praise has released.

HOW TO RELEASE SPIRITUAL POWER

Praise and the giving of thanks enable us to release the spiritual power that is within us. We are all filled with a dynamic force, whether we are aware of it or not. This dynamic force is spiritual power, and this power is constantly seeking release.

What the modern world often calls tension is nothing but man's spiritual power that has not found proper release and expression. Tense, nervous, and high-strung persons would have increased spiritual power and could do greater and more wonderful things if they consistently praised their minds, bodies, and affairs, for praise releases the inner spiritual power that lies within each of us.

A nurse from Pennsylvania wrote:

I have found the concepts of praise and thanksgiving especially beneficial to my emotional and intellectual states of mind. Oh! That I had had this knowledge years ago to help me overcome a most bleak existence.

However, in my present psychological state, maybe I can — in contrast — better appreciate the lessons learned now. Perhaps this is the divine timing for my enlightenment, at a period when I can see things in a clearer light.

Although there has been vast improvement, outwardly my life has not changed as much as I would like. But my 'life of the Spirit' is rich. Instead of feeling at the mercy of events and people, I feel more in control of my life now.

This Thanksgiving holiday I was off from my regular job. Instead of sitting home alone while everyone else seemed to have someone to be with, I decided to accept some "moon-lighting" assignments. I created a place to go by working when other nurses wanted a holiday. It has been a much happier time for me than it would have been had I remained at home remembering past hurts and feeling forgotten by my children. I am grateful for having learned about the power of praise and thanksgiving. This prayer practice has done wonders for me.

EVERYTHING RESPONDS TO PRAISE

Praise increases that to which it is directed. Praise draws and accumulates spiritual substance, and continual praise can bring forth prosperity. Praise draws and accumulates spiritual life, and continual praise can result in healing. Praise draws and accumulates knowledge, and it can bring forth guidance and help for any problem. *Praise can open a new, wonderful world to us, because praise draws and accumulates good and gives it power for expression.*

A businesswoman in California wrote:

> Here's how quickly the power of praise works: Last week we received two checks for work done, plus the gift of three days off. The weather is perfect, I have been healed, and all is beautiful again.
>
> I work with senior citizens and many come with pains and problems. But how wonderfully they respond to praise and thanksgiving. While I was finishing this letter, the mailman brought a letter which announced a pay raise for my husband. I praise God for all these blessings.

The whole creation responds to praise and is glad. We can praise our own ability, and our very brain cells will expand or increase in capacity when we speak to them words of encouragement and appreciation. When we feel discouraged, it is good to give ourselves a treatment in praise. This treatment changes our "I can't" attitudes and feelings so that they become "I can and I will" attitudes and feelings.

PRAISE STARTS US IN THE RIGHT DIRECTION

I recently heard someone compare an affirmation to a steering wheel in an auto. The steering wheel helps us to go in the right direction. Affirmations of praise also do this. They give us the desire to get started in the right direction and then they guide us on our way.

When we praise the riches or opulence of our loving Father, our mental atmosphere is greatly increased to receive these riches. Our wider mental outlook on riches opens the way for a richer supply. Through a persistent use of praise, a failing business can become a successful one, for even inanimate objects seem to respond to praise.

A woman once used the power of praise on her sewing machine, which was out of order. After she used words of praise, her sewing machine gave her no more trouble.

Another woman had a rag rug on her living room floor. For years she had been hoping for a new one. She heard of the law of praise and began to praise her old rug. Within two weeks a new one appeared from an unexpected source.

One of my associates recently related how the power of praise and blessing worked on a watch he was trying to repair. After he had done all that he could to repair the watch, my associate placed it on a shelf, blessed it, praised it, and left it for several days. When he inspected it later, he found that the watch ran perfectly.

BE SURE TO PRAISE OTHERS

We should praise the qualities we would like to see in others, declare that others possess them already, and then watch how quickly these persons will respond.

A housewife said, "Since I have adopted the praise method, there has been a great change in all my household. I no longer censure my help for apparent carelessness and for accidents, but I excuse the accident in some pleasant way and praise help for their good intentions, their faithfulness, and their goodness. Thus I call into activity the very qualities that I recognize, and I make them strong and potent and abiding."

A person often thinks, "*When* I have this or *when* I am able to do that, *then* I will be happy." But happiness does not come in these ways. Happiness already exists as a part of our divine nature. Through praise and thanksgiving we release this happiness.

OUR ATTITUDES AND WORDS AFFECT US: BOTH POSITIVELY AND NEGATIVELY

All of us are surrounded by a pulsating energy which Jesus called the kingdom of the heavens. Out of this universal energy we can form and make whatever we want. We can use this universal substance all the time to form and to make our world. When our thoughts are not the highest, we have to live with results that are not the best. But each of us has the spiritual power to form this pulsating, radiant substance into good in his mind, body, and affairs.

All our words and attitudes affect us. Every time we sing, pray, or praise, we are carrying out the creative law. If we would be successful and happy, we must be very careful how we talk or listen to others talk about failure. This can keep us from experiencing success. In like manner, if we want to experience health, we must praise health and bless it until it becomes apparent in our body temple. We should talk health to our children and to our associates.

It is by man's word of praise and blessing that his world is restored to its perfection.

A businessman in California wrote:

At a time when I was having financial problems, I faithfully declared words of praise and thanksgiving. Here were the results: The requested assistance of restitution for temporary losses in financial investments has been coming by leaps and bounds. Forgotten loans have been repaid. Investment returns have multiplied without interruption. I even have money left over now at the end of the month! We are using this to help pay for our daughter's education.

The Children of Israel were shown that their sufferings and afflictions came not because God willed them but because they were disobedient to the law of praise. In Deuteronomy we read: "All these curses shall come upon thee, and shall pursue thee, and overtake thee . . . Because thou servedst not Jehovah thy God with joyfulness, and with gladness of heart, by reason of the abundance of all things."[1] (Deuteronomy 28:45-47)

HOW TO REAP YOUR HARVEST OF INCREASED GOOD

The Bible records many instances where Jesus gave thanks. Before He multiplied the loaves and the fishes, He gave thanks. (Matthew 15:36) At the grave of Lazarus, He said, "Father, I thank thee that thou heardest me." (John 11:41) Note that He gave thanks *before* the answer appeared.

---

1. See the book *The Millionaire Moses* by Catherine Ponder, published (1977) by DeVorss & Co., Marina del Rey, Ca. 90291.

We can harvest our good through prayers of praise and thanksgiving, too. Our good awaits us, and through praise we make divine connection with it at just the right moment. Day by day we experience more and more of God's rich good through harvesting it with our thoughts and declarations of praise.

The way to have an abundant harvest of good is to render praise and thanksgiving for the good we are entitled to as spiritual beings, even *before* there is any sign of it. Another way to increase our harvest of good is to praise and give thanks for the good we already have. Try it! Such expressions of praise and thanksgiving can be among the most potent forms of prayer available to mankind.

PRAYER IN PICTURES

— Chapter 5 —

An engineer once shared with me his own private success formula, which brought forth great good for him.

This man began his study of the spiritual laws of prosperity and how to apply them in a practical manner at a time when he had just been told of a job transfer. The transfer created a series of problems. He realized from his Truth study that it would be necessary for him to develop and apply confidence and faith in God, in the spiritual laws of prosperity, and in himself, in order to work out all the details of his change successfully.

So he began to compile his own success formula. His first step was to regard God as a rich, loving, all-providing Father. He wrote God a series of letters listing his various problems and stating his human inability to handle them alone. Every time a new problem arose concerning the job transfer, he wrote God another letter and, as the solution to each problem unfolded, he wrote God letters of thanks. In this way he developed faith in God's goodness, and confidence in his own ability to work with God's prosperity laws of increase.

At this point he heard a lecture on the use of prayer in pictures. He became fascinated with this method as both practical and spiritual. However, he felt that something definite should be developed to inspire the average business person to use this powerful technique of prayer in pictures.

WHEEL OF FORTUNE DESIGNED FOR INDIVIDUAL PROSPERITY

So he prayerfully designed a "wheel of fortune" which he also used in solving his own prosperity problems. On a large piece of cardboard, he drew a circle. In the very center he placed a picture of Jesus Christ. This formed the innermost part of his wheel of fortune.

Then he divided his circle into six parts: *Spiritual growth, health, work, possessions, finances,* and *vacation.* In each of the sectors he placed pictures of the results he desired to achieve in those activities.

For instance, in the *business* sector he pasted a picture concerning the perfect job he hoped to find as a result of his forthcoming transfer. In connection with his pictures he used this affirmation: "I AM STIMULATED BY DIVINE INTELLIGENCE, IMPULSED BY DIVINE LOVE, AND GUIDED BY DIVINE POWER INTO MY RIGHT WORK, PERFORMING IT IN A PERFECT WAY FOR PERFECT PAY. THE DIVINE PLAN OF MY LIFE NOW TAKES SHAPE IN DEFINITE, CONCRETE EXPERIENCES, LEADING TO PERFECT HEALTH, HAPPINESS, SUCCESS, AND PROSPERITY."

In the *possessions* sector of his Wheel of Fortune, he pasted a picture of his present home, and with it, this affirmation: "Divine intelligence directs the right buyer to this property. Everyone concerned is blessed by a just and orderly exchange of values." Then, in the same space, he placed the picture of a new home, with the words, "INFINITE MIND KNOWS OUR NEED, KNOWS WHERE THE RIGHT HOUSE IS, AND KNOWS HOW TO MANIFEST IT TO US AT THE RIGHT TIME." To help his wife through the transition period of moving and readjustment, he placed her picture in this area too, in connection with this affirmation: "MY WIFE IS NOW STIMULATED BY DIVINE INTELLIGENCE, IMPULSED BY DIVINE LOVE, AND GUIDED BY DIVINE POWER, MANIFESTING IN HER EVERY EXPERIENCE PERFECT HEALTH, HAPPINESS, ABUNDANCE, AND SUCCESS." For their ability to go forth to new experiences in faith, there was a picture of a door, and the affirmation, "AS ONE DOOR CLOSES, A BIGGER AND BETTER DOOR OPENS."

In the *vacation* sector he attached the picture of a sandy beach and ocean background, with this prayer: "I GIVE THANKS FOR A DIVINELY PLANNED VACATION, UNDER DIVINELY PLANNED CONDITIONS, WITH DIVINELY PROVIDED SUPPLY." For his over-all prosperity he also added the affirmation, "I AM GUIDED BY INFINITE WISDOM, AND DIVINE ORDER IS ESTABLISHED IN MY FINANCES."

In the *spiritual growth* sector of the wheel, he affixed the picture of a church, in connection with which he wrote: "I AM GRATEFUL THAT FAITH ABIDES IN MY HEART, GROUNDED IN MY BELIEF THAT MY LIFE IS ONE WITH THE LIFE DIVINE. I AM DIVINELY GUIDED TO SPIRITUAL UNDERSTANDING AND DEVELOPMENT." Nearby, he also placed a picture of the Bible.

DEVELOPING CONFIDENCE IN GOD
AND YOURSELF THROUGH PICTURING

As this man's confidence in God and in himself developed, through daily letters to God, and through daily viewing his Wheel of Fortune and affirming the various prayers in connection with it, his problems gradually turned into happy solutions. He soon received an engineering appointment to a multi-million dollar construction job, with complete freedom of action, and responsibility only to the vice-president of the company.

He became so confident that their present home would be sold on time that he and his wife visited the new job location in a distant state and immediately found the ideal place to live. They set a date to return to the old home and move their furniture, a date by which they confidently expected the former home to be sold, and even went so far in faith as to make plane reservations for that date.

Everything worked out just as they had stipulated. Their house was sold on time and their furniture moved to their new home on the date they had set.

Then, after getting settled, they took a vacation in a lovely tropical area where there were sandy beaches and miles of ocean. When they returned, they were guided to a metaphysical church in their new location, as they had pictured it on their Wheel of Fortune.

This engineer truly proved the words of Goethe: "What you can do, or dream you can, begin it. Boldness has genius, power and magic in it." He further proved to himself, in working with the spiritual laws of prosperity, a fact that he already knew to be true in his engineering profession from working with blueprints: *results have to be planned. Prosperity is a planned result,* just as is every bridge that is built, every building that is constructed.

HOW THE WHEEL OF FORTUNE PRAYER METHOD TRANSFORMED HIS LIFE

Later, a friend of this engineer in Ohio reported to me how this same method led him from tragedy to happiness. He wrote:

Having been a tool and machine designer most of my life and having dealt in mathematics and cold facts, there is nothing of much use to me if it does not work. I have found and proven to myself that having unshakeable faith, a definite purpose or desire, and the willingness to abide with these principles plus the faith that God will work all things out for your good, are just as sound a formula as any mathematical, chemical or physical law. We do not stop to figure out why two plus two equals four every time we want to work a mathematical problem. We accept it with unmistakable faith. We also have to accept the laws of life in the same way.

I was first introduced to prayer through pictures by the engineer who was in Dr. Ponder's first prosperity class in Alabama in 1958—the class on which she based her best-selling book, *The Dynamic Laws of Prosperity.* This man went from a million-dollar construction job in Alabama to a fifteen-million dollar construction job in Ohio, as a result of the prayer-in-pictures method. He designed the Wheel of Fortune about which she has written in several of her books. It is a prayer method that has helped thousands.

When tragic experiences had brought me to my knees mentally, physically and financially, he suggested I, too, make a Wheel of Fortune.

The results?

I am now the most happy, contented, independent and prosperous of any time in my life! Many things began to happen right out of the blue that I previously wouldn't have believed were possible. Positions opened up at just the right time. Money began to flow my way. People became more helpful. Even parking spaces opened up at the right time. The prayer in pictures method works!

SUGGESTIONS FOR MAKING A
WHEEL OF FORTUNE

Although you will find specific instructions for making a Wheel of Fortune in my books, *The Dynamic Laws of Prosperity*, *The Healing Secret of the Ages*, *The Millionaires of Genesis*, and *Open Your Mind to Prosperity*, here are some suggestions that have been helpful to many people:

1. Use big, colorful poster boards for best results.

2. Use certain colors to obtain certain results: Green or gold for financial increase; orange for health; blue for intellectual achievement; pink for love and happiness; yellow for increased spiritual understanding.

3. Use colored pictures on your colored Wheel of Fortune since the mind responds quicker to color.

4. Do not clutter your Wheel of Fortune unless you want cluttered results. Instead

make several for the various phases of your life.

5. On your financial Wheel, place some pictures of money, not just the things you want—so that you may obtain them without indebtedness.

6. Place a spiritual symbol on your Wheel for divine protection.

7. Look at your Wheel daily and often for obtaining best results quicker.

8. Keep quiet about what you are picturing, so that you will not talk your good away.

PLAN YOUR PROSPERITY

Your good can also come forth as a planned result if you will write daily notes to God concerning your success, and then prayerfully construct your Wheel of Fortune and use it daily. When we visualize with the help of a Wheel of Fortune, we are really praying and imaging our good; we are changing the current of our thinking from negative to positive, from despair to hope, from discouragement to encouragement. *You can picture a thing and bring it through rather than trying to reason it through or force it through. You can hasten your good through picturing!* This is prayer in pictures at its best.

THE PRAYER OF INCREASE

— Chapter 6 —

Along with the use of definite verbal, silent and pictured prayers for increase (as described in previous chapters), the prayer of increase also works through: (1) attitudes of increase; and (2) a deliberate action that leads to increase.

PART I: ATTITUDES OF INCREASE

The use of attitudes of increase is simple and pleasant. It requires first the establishment and maintenance of an attitude of rich increase toward everybody and everything. Let your first thoughts, when thinking of others or contacting them by mail, by telephone, or in person, be thoughts and blessings of increase. Just thinking of a rich increase of good in connection with others helps them become more prosperous. They may not be consciously aware of your prosperous thoughts and blessings, but they will subconsciously receive them and be richly blessed.

Attitudes of increase are what all people are seeking to invoke in one way or another. The universal desire for increase is nothing more than man's innate divinity seeking expression as fuller good in his life. Every man instinctively feels it and instinctively responds to some extent. All people are seeking more or better food, clothes, homes, beauty, knowledge, leisure, pleasure, luxury—increase in something. And rightly so! *A normal desire for increased good is not to be condemned or suppressed. It is divine.*

BLESSING OTHERS BRINGS INCREASE

We should also convey the impression of increase with everything we do, so that others will receive that rich impression. The thought of blessing is the thought of increase. The prayer of increase releases it. Give this silent thought of increase, at every opportunity, to your family, social acquaintances, business associates, spiritual friends, world leaders, and all people everywhere: "I BLESS YOU AND BLESS YOU WITH A RICH INCREASE OF GOD'S ALMIGHTY GOOD."

When you bless people, inanimate objects, situations, and appearances with the thought of increased good, then that person, object, situation, or appearance unconsciously receives the good of your blessing. You are richer for having given it; it will come back to you as a richly multiplied blessing. And the recipient is richer for having had your attention and your prosperous thought. This practice is much more satisfying than the reverse, which too many people practice: thinking of things and people as failures.

BLESS YOURSELF WITH THE THOUGHT OF INCREASE

Another way to employ the attitude of increase is by blessing ourselves with an equal thought of increase. We can do this just by *feeling* that we are getting rich and that we are making others rich. Our every act, tone, and look should express a quiet, rich assurance. Words to convince others of our prosperity are not necessary when we get the feeling of richness implanted in our subconscious. The feeling can be radiated from us and communicated to others. They will then want to be associated with us in business transactions and otherwise, so as to benefit from our consciousness of prosperity.

A businesswoman said, "Prosperity started coming to me after I began to declare daily, "I CARRY MYSELF AS ONE WHO OWNS THE EARTH, FOR I DO!"

Another businesswoman, who had moved out of state on faith, found work, then got laid off. Instead of panicking, she told her children to dress up in their best clothes so she could take them out to dinner to celebrate the good that was on the way to them. As they all dwelled on thoughts of rich increase, she found a better job within two days.

Just by working quietly to attain a feeling of richness, we can draw to us prosperous-minded persons we have never seen before, who will become our customers and business associates. *People unconsciously go where there is a consciousness of increase.* It is thus that business increases rapidly, and many rich blessings flow to us. If we give the thought of increase to others and entertain it quietly in the deep recesses of our own minds, others are attracted to us and automatically help to prosper us.

SUCCESS IN YOUR WORK

Another way to invoke the attitude of increase is in regard to our work. We should do all that we can do every day, and we should do all of our work in an efficient manner. But the actual amount of work we do is not as important as our attitude about our work. Let us put the thought of success in everything we do.

If you do not feel that you are in your right place or in congenial work, practice using the attitude of increase anyway. As you bless others and yourself with the thought of increase, people, ideas, and opportunities will be attracted to you, and new channels of success and advancement will open to you.

PART II: A DELIBERATE ACTION THAT LEADS TO INCREASE

All of these mental attitudes are very important to prosperity. There is also something that we need to do in order to expand our faith in God as the source of our prosperity. This deliberate action leads to increased good on all levels of life: We should make Him our financial partner. *When we touch upon this par-*

ticular facet of the law of increase, our prosperity is constantly and divinely assured.

This facet of the prayer of increase is the spiritual act of tithing. Any practice that has been handed down through the centuries, as tithing has been, must have great importance. *Some persons may study other prosperity laws and be prospered for a time; but accomplishment is invariably easier and more lasting when the divine law of tithing is invoked.* Those who tithe associate themselves with divine riches; it is as though all forces of heaven and earth rush forth to guard, guide, and prosper them. Through tithing they go from success to greater success almost effortlessly, because they are divinely helped in their achieving.

In my own personal experience, prosperity proved elusive until I began tithing—at a time when I was making only $100 a month, supporting myself, my son, and helping another member of my family. Although I wondered, at first, if I could afford to tithe, I soon realized I could not afford *not* to tithe. The decision to tithe was not an easy one to make, but it was the wisest and most rewarding one I have ever made. The deliberate act of tithing consistently has gradually taken me from a life of limitation to one of fulfillment.

HOW THEY DEMONSTRATED ENOUGH
TO SPARE AND SHARE

Recently a jeweler said to me: "Before I began the practice of tithing, I could not make ends meet. Now I find that I have enough to spare and to share." Another man who heard this conversation said: "Since I decided to tithe I have never hesitated to get what I want and enjoy it. I used to wonder if I could afford certain things, and I often went without the very things I should have been enjoying as a child of God. Since beginning to tithe, I have purchased what I wanted in the way of homes, cars, and clothes, and always I've been enriched. The practice of tithing first made me feel rich, and then the outer riches came."

A postal employee reports: "A relative of mine has the same income as I do, but he's in constant financial need. Recently when I offered to help, he said, 'How can you possibly help me when your income is practically the same as mine?' I told him, 'The difference is that I tithe.' I think that if people would teach their children to tithe, the children would never have financial difficulties in later years."

A powerful prayer for daily use is: "VOLUNTARY, FAITHFUL TITHING OF MY WHOLE INCOME

BRINGS EVER-INCREASING PROSPERITY TO ME, AND
THROUGH ME TO OTHERS."

ONE PROBLEM AND ONE SOLUTION

People who have not learned of the benefits
derived from this special method of giving often
think that the way to prosper and succeed in life
is to hold tightly to everything they get. Yet, to
do so only leads to stagnation and congestion. It
blocks and stops their good.

Such people assume that the person who gives
generously and systematically in impersonal
ways will probably go broke; in any event, he is
very foolish. Yet the philosophers of all ages
have found that just the opposite is true: *Your
giving enriches you and expands your good on
all levels of life*. The sages of the past have said,
"There is only one problem in life: stagnation.
There is only one solution: circulation." To
observe the prospering power of tithing as it
works to bring about this circulation is a fasci-
nating process.

THE BROTHER WHO GAVE

There once were two brothers who practiced
these two divergent points of view: One tithed

and shared. The other did not. There was a striking difference in the results.

These brothers came from a poor family. Their father was a miser who would not voluntarily share even with his own children. They grew up under the belief that they must fight for everything they got in life; that they must cheat, scheme, and outwit everybody they met in order to prosper.

The eldest brother started out with nothing—not even an adequate education. He went to work early in life. While still in destitute circumstances, he began to practice giving and sharing. He worked hard at a menial job and helped his younger brother to get an education. After an impoverished childhood, in which so much had been needlessly withheld from him, it was a welcomed relief to this eldest brother to finally be freed to share. He never accepted his parent's limited attitudes that withholding would make one happy or successful in life.

In his studies toward self-improvement, he discovered this special method of giving that had been practiced since ancient times. He decided to invoke the power of increase by giving one-tenth of his gross income regularly to the New Thought church that had taught him that he could tithe and prosper. He knew it was an organization that was helping mankind through its teaching of universal truths.

His father and brother only shook their heads. "He will never make it because he gives away too much. He will go broke from all that 'foolish giving,' " they predicted.

THE BROTHER WHO WITHHELD

When the younger brother finished college, he married another college graduate from a "well-to-do" family, and "great things" were predicted for them. He did nothing to repay the eldest brother, who had struggled financially to help him get an education. His new wife resented the eldest brother's generosity, and all contact between them ceased. The younger brother adopted the attitude of his father that one could go broke by giving and sharing. He and his wife both worked, but they clutched everything. Nothing was voluntarily shared with others.

These two brothers were soon living on opposite sides of the continent. Because they had so little in common, there was no communication between them, and they did not see each other for more than two decades. The young brother's family wanted nothing to do with the eldest brother's family, whom they assumed had not "made it."

THE CONTRAST IN RESULTS

When these two brothers finally assembled for a family reunion, the contrast was striking:

The eldest brother—who started out with nothing, but who learned that giving and sharing are the beginning of increase—had become financially independent. His family enjoyed the vast benefits that their affluence made possible: a large home, a thriving business, private club memberships, prestige in the community, travel abroad, and good health.

The younger brother, who had started out with a fine education and a well-to-do wife to help him, but who had held on tightly to everything—the one for whom "great things" had been predicted—was anything but affluent. Heavily in debt, he was living beyond his means in an effort to appease his ambitious family. He was plagued by the related pressures of ill health and family problems. Since none of his family had learned the inner laws of success, none of them were successful, either. At best, this entire family was leading a negative, frustrated, limited way of life. They felt hemmed in as they continued to talk financial lack. *By clinging to the little things in life, they had held themselves in limitation.* They had no hope for a better way of life.

After the relatives got over the shock of the eldest brother's affluence, they reluctantly asked the secret of his success. He laughingly replied, "The secret of my success is all of the 'foolish giving' that you criticized me for twenty years ago. I have faithfully tithed ten percent of my income to my church, and I have shared generously in countless other ways. Since giving is the beginning of financial increase, I have shared my way to success."

The relatives he had not seen for twenty years only shook their heads. They still were not ready to open their minds and share. They sadly said to each other, "When will he ever learn to stop all that 'foolish giving'?"

Solomon explained the benefits of such "foolish giving" when he promised:

> There is that which scattered, yet increases the more. And there is that which is withheld more than is meet, but tendeth only to want. The liberal soul shall be blessed. And he that watereth shall be watered also himself.
>
> (Proverbs 11:24,25)

The younger brother proved that *when any person withholds that which belongs to the universe, his life is thrown out of balance*. The eldest brother proved that *it is only as we let go of our littleness that we can expand into the larger life.*

WHERE YOU GIVE
AFFECTS YOUR PROSPERITY

A merchant in the furniture business recently told me that he had tithed at various times without satisfactory results; and that it was only after he heard a lecture on the importance of tithing to the spiritual organization or person from which one receives spiritual help, that he realized why he had not previously prospered. He had been tithing to a certain church to please his family, although he was not receiving the inspiration he needed from that church. He began tithing to the spiritual organization that was inspiring him — and the prosperous results in his business have reflected the change.

See SPECIAL NOTE FROM THE AUTHOR, next page.

AN IMPORTANT NOTE
FROM THE AUTHOR

Through the generous outpouring of their tithes over the years, readers of my books have helped me financially to establish three new churches—the most recent being a global ministry, the nondenominational *Unity Church Worldwide,* with headquarters in Palm Desert, California. Many thanks for your help in the past and for all you continue to share.

You are also invited to share your tithes with the churches of your choice—especially those that teach the truths stressed in this book. Such churches include the nondenominational churches of Unity, Centers for Spiritual Living (Science of Mind / Religious Science), Divine Science, and others that are related, many of which are part of the International New Thought Movement. For more information you can visit their website at www.newthoughtalliance.org, or mail you inquiry to The International New Thought Alliance, 5003 E. Broadway Road, Mesa, AZ 85206. Your support of churches such as these can help spread the prosperous Truth that humanity is now seeking.

To contact Catherine Ponder or her UNITY CHURCH WORLDWIDE ministry for prayer help, literature, or other reasons, you may reach her at P.O. Drawer 1278, Palm Desert, CA 92261 USA.